The Wit and Wisdom of Joseph Biden

By Publius

"Let me start off with two words: Made in America"

— remarks of 10/7/22

Published by [Parker Publishers]

Cover design by [Parker Publishers]

Printed in [USA]

TABLE OF CONTENTS

About The Author iv

Preface: Can't Walk A Line v

The Wit and Wisdom 1

ABOUT THE AUTHOR

Publius is best known for his writing of The Federalist Papers, a series of 85 essays which promoted the ratification of the Constitution of the United States between October 1787 and May 1788, published in various New York state newspapers of the time.

Although he has not published anything new until now, with the sagacity and perspective he has gained as he approaches his three hundredth birthday, Publius has decided that our current political crisis requires careful review and thought about the leading contenders for the presidency in 2024.

Accordingly, Publius has spent more than two years reviewing all the speeches, writings, tweets, press releases, rallies, and utterances of the 45th and 46th U.S. Presidents, including a complete review of classified documents stored in the bathroom at Mar-a-Lago.

From this exhaustive review, Publius has compiled comprehensive lists of the learned and insightful thoughts from these men who are indisputably the two greatest Americans of the current time, and perhaps the greatest since the Founding Fathers.

Now available for the first time to the general public, Publius' two groundbreaking companion books, The Wit and Wisdom of Donald Trump and The Wit and Wisdom of Joseph Biden, should be read by everyone as they consider their vote in 2024.

Preface

Can't Walk A Line (to the tune of "I Walk The Line" by Johnny Cash

My doctor worries 'bout this heart of mine,
I shut my eyes, fall asleep all the time,
I keep on talking though my mind unwinds,
I am not fine, can't walk a line.

I find it very, very hard to stay awake,
Nothing is true that I say, it's all fake,
I cannot speak at all, for goodness sake,
I am not fine, can't walk a line.

As sure as night is dark and day is light,
My mind is addled in both day and night,
And I will never do anything right,
I am not fine, can't walk a line.

I don't know how to get you on my side,
I've done some bad things that I hope to hide,
Before my term's over, I might have died,
I am not fine, can't walk a line.

My doctor worries 'bout this heart of mine,
I shut my eyes, fall asleep all the time,
I keep on talking though my mind unwinds,
I am not fine, can't walk a line

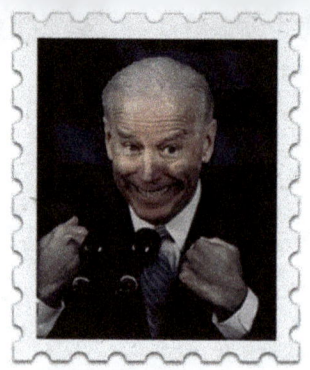

The Wit and Wisdom

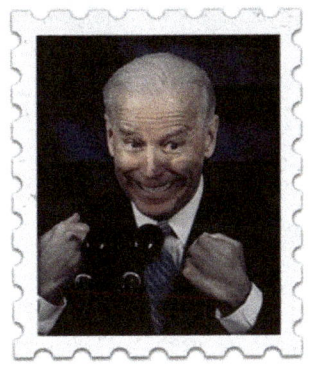

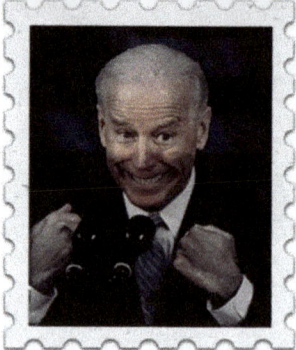

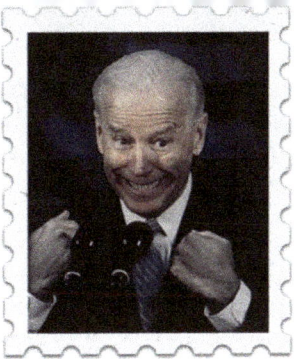

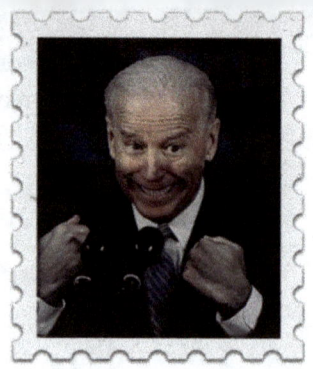

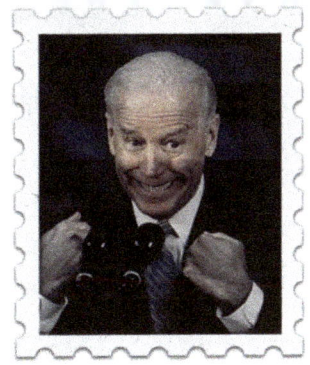

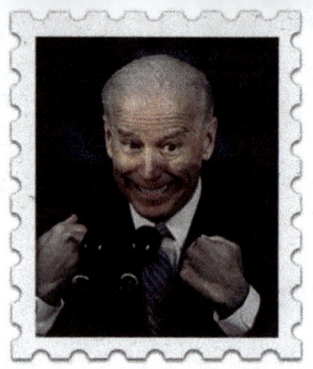

The Wit and Wisdom of Joseph Biden

The Wit and Wisdom of Joseph Biden

The Wit and Wisdom of Joseph Biden

The Wit and Wisdom of Joseph Biden

The Wit and Wisdom of Joseph Biden

The Wit and Wisdom of Joseph Biden

The Wit and Wisdom of Joseph Biden

The Wit and Wisdom of Joseph Biden

The Wit and Wisdom of Joseph Biden

.

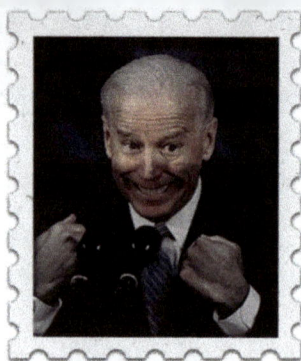

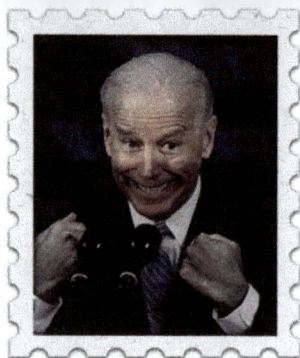

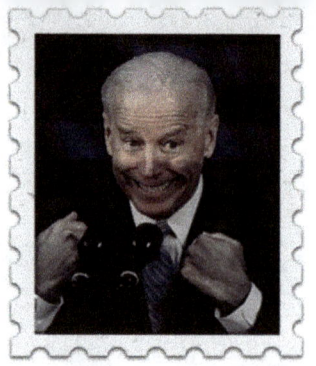

The Wit and Wisdom of Joseph Biden

The Wit and Wisdom of Joseph Biden

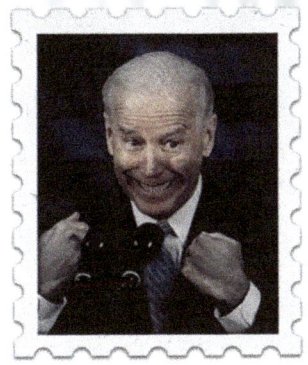

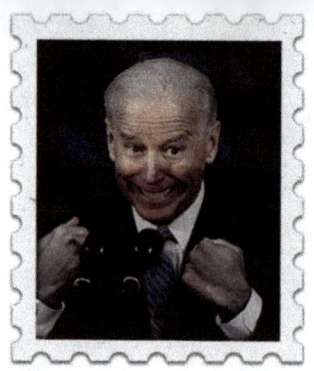

The Wit and Wisdom of Joseph Biden

The Wit and Wisdom of Joseph Biden

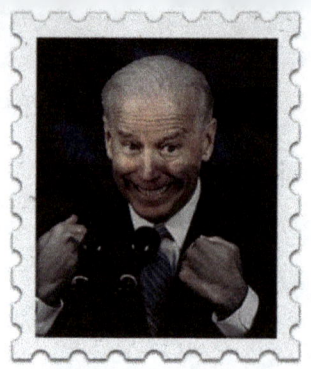

The End.

Printed in the USA
CPSIA information can be obtained
at www.ICGtesting.com
LVHW081236070324
773597LV00007B/130

9 787584 479354